To _____

From _____

Our world is filled with tenderness,
   and it's people like you
Who make it that way
   by the things that you do.
For a warm, ready smile
   or a kind, thoughtful deed
Or a hand outstretched
   in an hour of need
Can change the whole outlook
   and make the world bright,
Where a minute before
   just nothing seemed right.

The Helen Steiner Rice Foundation

Whatever the celebration, whatever the day, whatever the event, whatever the occasion, Helen Steiner Rice possessed the ability to express the appropriate feeling for that particular moment.

A happening became happier, a sentiment more sentimental, a memory more memorable because of her deep sensitivity and ability to put into understandable language the emotion being experienced. Her positive attitude, her concern for others, and her love of God are identifiable threads woven into her life, her work . . . and even her death.

Prior to Mrs. Rice's passing, she established the Helen Steiner Rice Foundation, a nonprofit corporation that awards grants to worthy charitable programs assisting the elderly and the needy. In her lifetime, these were the individuals about whom Mrs. Rice was greatly concerned.

Royalties from the sale of this book will add to the financial capabilities of the Helen Steiner Rice Foundation. Because of limited resources, the foundation presently limits grants to qualified charitable programs in Lorain, Ohio, where Helen Steiner Rice was born, and Greater Cincinnati, Ohio, where Mrs. Rice lived and worked most of her life. Hopefully in the future, resources will be of sufficient size that broader geographical areas may be considered in the awarding of grants. Thank you for your assistance in helping to keep Helen's dreams alive.

Andrea R. Cornett, Administrator

John Ruthven, internationally acknowledged master of wildlife art, has won numerous national and international awards for his paintings. The founder of Wildlife Internationale, Inc., he has won the prestigious Federal Duck Stamp design competition.

Eyes of Tenderness

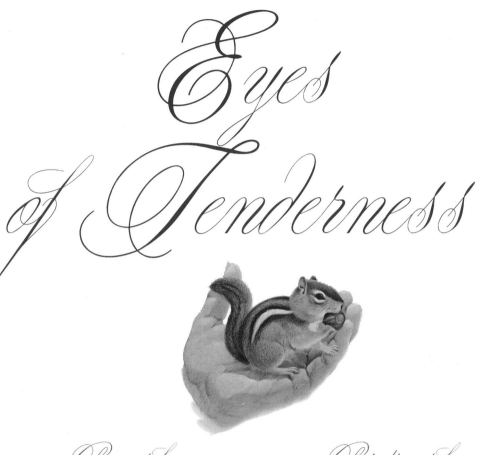

Poems by
HELEN STEINER RICE

Paintings by
JOHN A. RUTHVEN

Compiled by Virginia J. Ruehlmann

Fleming H. Revell
A Division of Baker Book House Co
Grand Rapids, Michigan 49516

Published by Fleming H. Revell
a division of Baker Book House Company
P.O. Box 6287, Grand Rapids, Michigan 49516-6287

Printed in the United States of America

Library of Congress Cataloging-in-Publication Data

Rice, Helen Steiner.
    Eyes of tenderness / poems by Helen Steiner Rice ;
paintings by John A. Ruthven ; compiled by Virginia J.
Ruehlmann.
        p.   cm.
    ISBN 0-8007-1737-6 (cloth)
    1. Christian poetry, American. I. Ruthven, John A.
II. Ruehlmann, Virginia J. III. Title.
PS3568.I28E95   1997
811'.54—dc21   96-37889

Contents

Dedicated to
Judy and John A. Ruthven,
who epitomize the quality
of tenderness,
possess its inherent attributes,
and practice it in
their daily lives
through kind words,
encouraging actions,
and sincere appreciation
of all the creations
and creatures of God.

Introduction

In whatever season or setting, be it

winter, as you gaze through a window, admiring the beauty of freshly fallen snow punctuated with paw prints and treasuring the intrigue of identifying the tracks made by chipmunks, raccoons, and squirrels;

spring, as you walk through a garden, observing the miraculous signs of new life in the appearance of tulips, butterflies, baby rabbits, hyacinths, and robins' eggs;

summer, as you relax at the edge of a crystal-clear lake while relishing the many wonders of life highlighted by sunrises, sunsets, cotton-like clouds drifting by while ducks, geese, and fish enjoy the cool water;

autumn, as you climb majestic mountains or hike in color-bedecked woods and appreciate nature's panoramic scenes while identifying various forms of wildlife,

you have opportunities to discover happiness and contentment. Invariably, in doing so, you also have the privilege of cherishing the quality of tenderness. You can relate to this much-admired attribute when each scene and every moment are appreciated. Tenderness can be observed in God's creatures—animals, birds, water fowl, and humans.

Helen Steiner Rice possessed the uncanny ability of uncovering tenderness in various situations and, using her God-given talent, expressed it in a beautiful, poetic style. Artist-naturalist John A. Ruthven, adept at spotting tender happenings in the out-of-doors, interprets such scenes through his innate talent and the tools of his profession.

May the efforts of Rice and Ruthven assist you in discovering the presence of tenderness in the natural surroundings of life.

Tenderly,
Virginia J. Ruehlmann

Compassion

*T*eddy was my dog, and he would do anything for me. He waited for me to come home from school. He slept beside me, and when I whistled he ran to me even if he were eating. . . . And so when I went away to war, I did not know how to leave him. How do you explain to someone who loves you that you are leaving him.

So, coming home from the navy that first time was something I can scarcely describe. . . . It was two or three in the morning before I was within half a mile of the house. . . . Suddenly Teddy heard me and began his warning barking. Then I whistled—only once. The barking stopped. There was a yelp of recognition. . . . Almost immediately he was there in my arms. To this day, that is the best way I can explain what I mean by "coming home."

David Redding

I believe that man will not merely endure; he will prevail. He is immortal, not because he alone among creatures has an inexhaustible voice, but because he has a soul, a spirit capable of compassion and sacrifice and endurance.

William Faulkner

Focus on Friendship

Among the great and glorious gifts
    our Heavenly Father sends
Is the gift of understanding
    that we find in loving friends.
For somehow in the generous heart
    of loving, faithful friends,
Our good God in His charity
    and wisdom always sends
A sense of understanding
    and the power of perception
And mixes these fine qualities
    with kindness and affection.
So when we need some sympathy
    or a friendly hand to touch
Or one who listens tenderly
    and speaks words that mean so much,
We seek a true and trusted friend
    in the knowledge that we'll find
A heart that's sympathetic
    and an understanding mind,
And often just without a word
    there seems to be a union
Of thoughts and kindred feelings,
    for God gives true friends communion.

Generosity

Into our lives come many things
    to break the dull routine,
The things we had not planned on
    that happen unforeseen—
The unexpected little joys
    that are scattered on our way,
Success we did not count on
    or a rare, fulfilling day,
An unsought word of kindness,
    a compliment or two
That set the eyes to gleaming
    like crystal drops of dew,
The sudden, unplanned meeting
    that comes with sweet surprise
And lights the heart with happiness
    like a rainbow in the skies.
Now some folks call it fickle fate
    and some folks call it chance
While others just accept it
    as a pleasant happenstance,
But no matter what you call it,
    it didn't come without design,
For all our lives are fashioned
    by the hand that is divine,
And every lucky happening
    and every lucky break
Are little gifts from God above
    that are ours to freely take.

Somebody Cares

Somebody cares and always will,
The world forgets, but God loves you still.
You cannot go beyond His love
No matter what you're guilty of,
For God forgives until the end—
He is your faithful, loyal friend,
And though you try to hide your face,
There is no shelter anyplace
That can escape His watchful eye,
For on the earth and in the sky,
He's ever present and always there
To take you in His tender care
And bind the wounds and mend the breaks
When all the world around forsakes.
Somebody cares and loves you still,
And God is the Someone who always will.

You Too Must Weep

Let me not live a life that's free
From the things that draw me close to Thee,
For how can I ever hope to heal
The wounds of others I do not feel?
If my eyes are dry and I never weep,
How do I know when the hurt is deep?
If my heart is cold and never bleeds,
How can I tell what my brother needs?
For when ears are deaf to the beggar's plea
And we close our eyes and refuse to see
And we steel our hearts and harden our minds
And we count it a weakness whenever we're kind,
We are no longer following the Father's way
Or seeking His guidance from day to day.
So spare me no heartache or sorrow, dear Lord,
For the heart that hurts reaps the richest reward,
And God blesses the heart that is broken with sorrow
As He opens the door to a brighter tomorrow—
For only through tears can we recognize
The suffering that lies in another's eyes.

So We Might Know

Perhaps this is a vision
  of what true love can be
When it's fashioned out of sweetness
  and tender sympathy,
For such love has all the qualities
  of an eternal light
That keeps the garments of the soul
  clean and pure and bright.
And do not think this shadow
  was the herald of the night,
But an ambassador of love,
  that maketh all things right.

Confidence

There were four little foxes; and they looked curiously like lambs, with their wooly coats, their long, thick legs and their innocent expressions, and yet a second glance at their broad, sharp-nosed, sharp-eyed visages showed that each of these innocents was the making of a crafty old fox. They played about, basking in the sun, or wrestling with each other till a slight sound made them scurry under cover. But their alarm was needless, for the cause of it was their mother. . . . A low call from her and the little fellows came tumbling out. . . . The mother, keeping a sharp eye for enemies, looked on with fond delight. . . . Over all was the unmistakable look of the mother's pride and love.

Ernest Seton-Thompson

I can better trust those who helped to relieve the gloom of my dark hours than those who are so ready to enjoy with me the sunshine of my prosperity.

Ulysses S. Grant

See the Dew Glisten

The earth is the Lord's,
    and the fullness thereof,"
It speaks of His greatness,
    it sings of His love.
And each day at dawning,
    I lift my heart high
And raise up my eyes
    to the infinite sky.
I see the dew glisten
    in crystal-like splendor
While God, with a touch
    that is gentle and tender,
Wraps up the night
    and softly tucks it away
And hangs out the sun
    to herald a new day—
A day yet unblemished
    by what's gone before,
A chance to begin
    and start over once more.

There Is a Reason for Everything

Our Father knows what's best for us,
    so why should we complain?
We always want the sunshine,
    but He knows there must be rain.
We love the sound of laughter
    and the merriment of cheer,
But our hearts would lose their tenderness
    if we never shed a tear.
Our Father tests us often
    with suffering and with sorrow.
He tests us not to punish us
    but to help us meet tomorrow,
For growing trees are strengthened
    when they withstand the storm,
And the sharp cut of a chisel
    gives the marble grace and form.
So whenever we are troubled
    and when everything goes wrong,
It is just God working in us
    to make our spirits strong.

Open Our Eyes and Hearts

It's a wonderful world,
and it always will be
If we keep our eyes open
and focused to see
The wonderful things
we are capable of
When we open our hearts
to God and His love.

Are You Dissatisfied with Yourself?

We are often discontented and much dissatisfied
That our wish for recognition has not been gratified.
We feel that we've been cheated in beauty, charm, and brains,
And we think of all our losses and forget about our gains.
And dwelling on the things we lack we grow miserable inside,
Brooding on our deficits that are born of selfish pride.
We begin to harbor hatred, and envy fills our hearts
Because we do not possess the things that make others seem so smart.
And in our condemnation of the traits that we possess,
We magnify our painful plight and sink deeper in distress.
Oh, Lord, forgive our foolishness, our vanity and pride
As we strive to please the eye of man and not God, who sees inside,
And little do we realize how contented we would be
If we knew that we are beautiful when our hearts are touched by Thee.

Look Ahead

Looking ahead, the hills seem steep
  and the road rises up to the sky,
But as we near them and start to climb,
  they never seem half as high.
And thinking of work and trouble,
  we worry and hesitate,
But just as soon as we tackle the job,
  the burden becomes less great.
So whether a hill, a task or load,
  a minute, an hour, a day,
As we grow near it and start to climb,
  easier grows the way.

God's Tender Touch

When trouble comes,
   as it does to us all,
God is so great,
   and we are so small,
But there is nothing
   that we need know
If we have faith
   wherever we go
That God will be waiting
   to help us bear
Our pain and sorrow,
   our suffering and care,
For no pain or suffering
   is ever too much
To yield itself
   to God's tender touch.

Encouragement

We walked to the edge of the precipice and looked over the lip down at the black rocks and tumult of torn surf below. Among broken islands, the white water formed a seething caldron. And there, just below us, as though sporting in a millpond, two magnificent . . . otters played in the storm of waters. They rolled over and over, twining and intertwining, diving and being tossed aloft, floating on their backs with head and feet in the air, swimming side by side with noses touching. They seemed unaware of the towering breakers that were thundering on the rocks and exploding all around them.

Edwin Way Teale

I consider my ability to arouse enthusiasm among men the greatest asset I possess, and the way to develop the best that is in a man is by appreciation and encouragement.

Charles Schwab

Tender Thoughts

No day is unmeetable
    if, on rising, your first thought
Is to thank God for the blessings
    that His tender care has brought,
For there can be no failures
    or hopeless, unsaved sinners
If you enlist the help of God,
    who makes all losers winners,
And if you follow faithfully
    this daily way to pray,
You will never in your lifetime
    face another hopeless day.

Daily Prayers Dissolve All Cares

Meet God in the morning
   and take Him with you through the day,
And then before you go to sleep
   do not forget to pray
That He will just take over
   all the problems you couldn't solve,
And in the peacefulness of sleep
   your cares will all dissolve,
And when you open up your eyes
   to greet another day,
You'll find yourself renewed in strength
   and there will open up a way
To meet what seemed impossible
   for you to solve alone,
And once again you'll be assured
   you're never on your own.
So meet Him in the morning,
   keep Him with you through the day,
And thank Him for His guidance
   each evening when you pray.

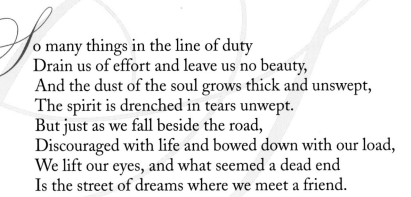

Discouragement and Dreams

So many things in the line of duty
Drain us of effort and leave us no beauty,
And the dust of the soul grows thick and unswept,
The spirit is drenched in tears unwept.
But just as we fall beside the road,
Discouraged with life and bowed down with our load,
We lift our eyes, and what seemed a dead end
Is the street of dreams where we meet a friend.

Climb Till Your Dream Comes True

Often your tasks will be many,
    and more than you think you can do.
Often the road will be rugged,
    and the hills insurmountable too.
But always remember the hills ahead
    are never as steep as they seem,
And with faith in your heart, start upward
    and climb till you reach your dream.
For nothing in life that is worthy
    is ever too hard to achieve
If you have the courage to try it
    and you have the faith to believe,
For faith is a force that is greater
    than knowledge or power or skill,
And many defeats turn to triumphs
    if you trust in God's wisdom and will.
Faith is a mover of mountains—
    there's nothing that God cannot do—
So start out today with faith in your heart
    and climb till your dream comes true.

Moments of Meditation

When your nervous network
 becomes a tangled mess,
Just close your eyes in silent prayer
 and ask the Lord to bless
Each thought that you are thinking,
 each decision you must make,
As well as every word you speak
 and every step you take,
For only by the grace of God
 can you gain self-control,
And only meditative thoughts
 can restore your peace of soul.

Patience

The chickadees we have always with us. They are like the evergreens among the trees and plants. Winter has no terrors for them. They are properly wood-birds, but the groves and orchards know them also. . . . Branch-builders and ground-builders are easily accommodated, but the chickadee must find a cavity, and a small one at that. . . . This a pair did a few yards from my cabin. The opening was into the heart of a little sassafras, about four feet from the ground. Day after day the birds took turns in deepening and enlarging the cavity: a soft, gentle hammering for a few moments in the heart of the little tree, and then the appearance of the worker at the opening, with the chips in his, or her, beak. They changed off every little while, one working while the other gathered food.

John Burroughs

In all things, from childhood's little troubles to the martyr's sufferings, patience is the grace of God, whereby we endure evil for the love of God.

Edward B. Pusey

Swift the Way and Short the Day

In this fast-moving world of turmoil and tension
With problems and troubles too many to mention,
Our days are so crowded and our hours are so few—
There's so little time and so much to do.
Sometimes we wonder as we rush through the day,
Does God really want us to hurry this way?
Why are we impatient and continually vexed
And often bewildered, disturbed, and perplexed?
Perhaps we're too busy with our own selfish seeking
To hear the dear Lord when He's tenderly speaking.
But God in His mercy looks down on us all,
And though what we've done may be pitifully small,
He makes us feel welcome to reflect and to pray
For the chance to do better as we start a new day,
For life would be better if we learned to rely
On our Father in heaven without asking why,
And if we'd remember as we rush through the day,
The Lord is our Shepherd and He'll lead the way.
So don't rush ahead in reckless endeavor,
Remember He leadeth, and time is forever.

The Gift of Lasting Love

Love is much more than a tender caress
And more than bright hours of glad happiness,
For a lasting love is made up of sharing
Both hours that are joyous and also despairing.
It's made up of patience and deep understanding
And never of stubborn or selfish demanding.
It's made up of climbing the steep hills together
And facing with courage life's stormiest weather.
For nothing on earth or in heaven can part
A love that has grown to be part of the heart.

This Is Just a Resting Place

Sometimes the road of life seems long
    as we travel through the years,
And with hearts that are broken
    and eyes brimful of tears,
We falter in our weariness
    and sink beside the way,
But God leans down and whispers,
    "Child, there'll be another day."
And the road will grow much smoother
    and much easier to face,
So do not be disheartened—
    this is just a resting place.

Strangers Are Friends We Haven't Met

God knows no strangers, He loves us all—
The poor, the rich, the great, the small.
He is a friend who is always there
To share our troubles and lessen our care,
For no one is a stranger in God's sight,
For God is love, and in His light
May we too try in our small way
To make new friends from day to day.
So pass no stranger with an unseeing eye,
For God may be sending a new friend by.

Secure in God's Love

Just close your eyes
  and open your heart
And feel your cares
  and worries depart.
Just yield yourself
  to the Father above
And let Him hold you
  secure in His love.

Protection

Although from the great and strong we have to apprehend danger, the feeble and apparently insignificant may have it in their power to annoy us beyond endurance. Even the bravest of our boasting race is, by this little animal, compelled suddenly to . . . hold his nose, and run—as if a lion were at his heels.

Among the first specimens of natural history we attempted to procure was the skunk, in our early schoolboy days. We observed in the path before us a pretty little animal, playful as a kitten, moving quietly along. . . . What a pretty creature to carry home in our arms! Let us catch it. . . . We seize it with the energy of a miser clutching a bag of diamonds. A short struggle ensues, when—faugh! we are suffocated. We drop our prize and take to our heels, too stubborn to cry, but too much alarmed to take another look.

John Audubon

Perhaps the most amazing example of mother love is the superb courage of animals in giving protection when dangers arise.

Alan Devoe

The Peace of Meditation

Our Father tells His children that if they would know His will,
They must seek Him in the silence when all is calm and still,
For nature's great forces are found in quiet things
Like softly falling snowflakes drifting down on angels' wings
Or petals dropping soundlessly from a lovely full-blown rose—
So God comes closest to us when our souls are in repose.
So let us plan with prayerful care to always allocate
A certain portion of each day to be still and meditate,
For when everything is quiet and we're lost in meditation,
Our souls are then preparing for a deeper dedication
That will make it wholly possible to quietly endure
The violent world around us, for in God we are secure.

A Steppingstone to Growth

Whatever this year has in store,
Remember there's good reason for
Everything that comes into our life,
For even in times of struggle and strife
If we but lift our eyes above,
We see our challenge as a gift of love,
For things that cause the heart to ache
Until we feel that it must break
Become the strength by which we climb
To higher heights that are sublime.
So welcome every stumbling block
And every thorn and jagged rock,
For each one is a steppingstone
To a fuller life than we've ever known,
And in the radiance of God's smiles
We learn to persevere through life's trials.

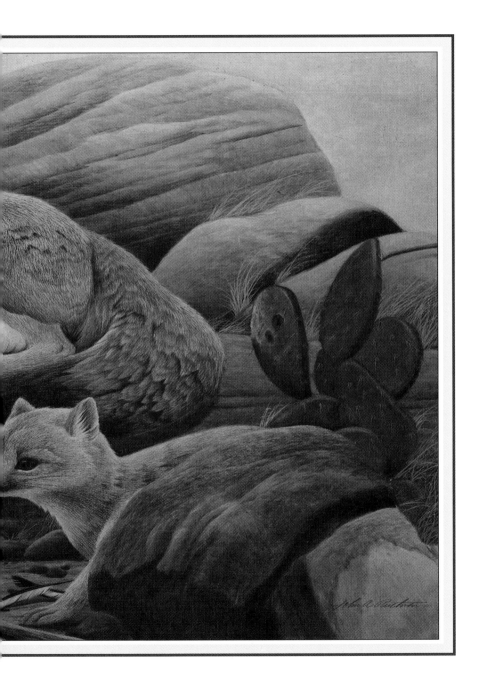

Triumph over Trouble

If wishes worked like magic,
  and plans worked that way too,
And everything you wished for,
  whether good or bad for you,
Immediately was granted
  with no effort on your part,
You'd experience no fulfillment
  of your spirit or your heart,
For things achieved too easily
  lose their charm and meaning too,
For it is life's difficulties
  and the trials we go through

That make us strong in spirit
   and endow us with the will
To surmount the insurmountable
   and to climb the highest hill.
So wish not for the easy way
   to win your heart's desire,
For the joy's in overcoming
   and withstanding flood and fire,
For to triumph over trouble
   and grow stronger with defeat
Is to win the kind of victory
   that will make your life complete.

After the Winter, the Spring

Springtime is a season
   of hope and joy and cheer.
There's beauty all around us
   to see and touch and hear.
So no matter how downhearted
   and discouraged we may be,
New hope is born when we behold
   leaves budding on a tree
Or when we see a timid flower
   push through the frozen sod
And open wide in glad surprise
   its petaled eyes to God,
For this is just God saying,
   "Lift up your eyes to Me,
And the bleakness of your spirit,
   like the budding springtime tree,
Will lose its wintry darkness
   and your heavy heart will sing"—
For God never sends the winter
   without the joy of spring.

Serenity

Occasionally one or several pair of wild trumpeter swans come in to land on the lake. Of all our feathered friends, they are the most noble and regal. Their graceful forms and immaculate white plumage grace the blue waters in resplendent contrast.

The other morning I watched a pair wheel proudly over the lake. Even their flight was grand and stately. They moved in wondrous unison, like a pair of superb ballet dancers in a sublime pas de deux. . . .

With majestic beauty, they circled down into the mist, their flowing forms gradually melding into the enveloping whiteness. It was as if they had vanished into vapor, passing silently yet serenely from life into death.

It was a poignant pageantry. It had lasted but a few fleeting moments. It had been observed only by one man. But, as with so many of God's great gifts, the man was richer for having gladly received it.

W. Phillip Keller

The gift of yourself to someone who needs you will, in return, bring the gift of confidence and serenity to you.

John H. Crowe

Steady My Gaze

Take me and break me and make me, dear God,
    just what You want me to be.
Give me the strength to accept what You send
    and eyes with the vision to see
All the small, arrogant ways that I have
    and the vain little things that I do,
Make me aware that I'm often concerned
    more with myself than with You.
Uncover before me my weakness and greed
    and help me to search deep inside,
So I may discover how easy it is
    to be selfishly lost in my pride.
And then in Thy goodness and mercy,
    look down on this weak, erring one
And tell me that I am forgiven
    for all I've so willfully done,
And teach me to humbly start following
    the path that the dear Savior trod,
So I'll find at the end of life's journey
    a home in the city of God.

A Proper View

When life seems empty and there's no place to go,
When your heart is troubled and your spirits are low,
When friends seem few and nobody cares—
There is always God to hear your prayers.
And whatever you're facing will seem much less
When you go to God and confide and confess,
For the burden that seems too heavy to bear,
God lifts away on the wings of prayer.
And seen through God's eyes, earthly troubles diminish
And we're given new strength to face and to finish
Life's daily tasks as they come along
If we pray for the strength to keep us strong.

Seek His Guidance

Refuse to be discouraged,
   refuse to be distressed,
For when we are despondent,
   our lives cannot be blessed—
For doubt and fear and worry
   close the door to faith and prayer,
And there's no room for blessings
   when we're lost in deep despair.
So remember when you're troubled
   with uncertainty and doubt,
It is best to tell our Father
   what our fear is all about—
For unless we seek His guidance
   when troubled times arise,
We are bound to make decisions
   that are twisted and unwise,
But when we view our problems
   through the eyes of God above,
Misfortunes turn to blessings
   and hatred turns to love.

A Prayer of Comfort

Take the Savior's loving hand
And do not try to understand,
Just let Him lead you where He will,
Through pastures green and waters still,
And though the way ahead seems steep,
Be not afraid for He will keep
Tender watch through night and day,
And He will hear each prayer you pray.
So place yourself in His loving care,
And He will gladly help you bear
Whatever lies ahead of you,
For there is nothing God can't do.

Silently

Silently the green leaves grow,
In silence falls the soft, white snow.
Silently the flowers bloom,
In silence sunshine fills a room.
Silently bright stars appear,
In silence velvet night draws near.
And silently God enters in
To free a troubled heart from sin,
For God works silently in lives,
For nothing spiritual survives
Amid the din of a noisy street
Where raucous crowds with hurrying feet
And blinded eyes and deafened ears
Are never privileged to hear
The message God wants to impart
To every troubled, weary heart.
So let not our worldly celebrations
Disturb our peaceful meditations,
For only in a quiet place
Can we behold God face to face.

Today's Joy

Who said the darkness of the night
    would never turn to day?
Who said the winter's bleakness
    would never pass away?
Why should we ever entertain
    these thoughts so dark and grim
And let the brightness of our minds
    grow cynical and dim,
When we know beyond all questioning
    that winter turns to spring
And on the notes of sorrow
    new songs are made to sing?
For no one sheds a teardrop
    or suffers loss in vain,
For God is always there to turn
    our losses into gain . . .
And every burden borne today
    and every present sorrow
Are but God's happy harbingers
    of a joyous, bright tomorrow.

Reflective Thoughts

Everybody everywhere, no matter what his station,
Has moments of deep loneliness and quiet desperation,
For this lost and lonely feeling is inherent in mankind,
It is just the spirit speaking as God tries again to find
An opening in the worldly wall man builds against God's touch,
For he feels so sufficient that he doesn't need God much,
So he vainly goes on struggling to find some explanation
For these disturbing, lonely moods of inner isolation.
But the answer keeps eluding him, for in his finite mind,
He does not even recognize that he will never find
The reason for life's emptiness unless he learns to share
The problems and the burdens that surround him everywhere,
But when his eyes are opened and he really looks at others,
He begins to see not strangers but people who are brothers.
So open up your hardened hearts and let God enter in,
He only wants to help you a new life to begin,
And every day's a good day to lose yourself in others,
And any time's a good time to see mankind as brothers,
And this can only happen when you realize it's true
That everyone needs someone and that "someone" is you.

Togetherness

The Canada goose is an unusually wary and intelligent bird. The social behavior within any given flock is complex, tightly knit and fiercely maintained. The birds are exceedingly loyal to each other and to their young. The interrelationship of the birds is maintained by almost-continuous conversation, which I call "goose gossip."

W. Phillip Keller

No possession is gratifying without a companion.

Seneca

John A. Ruthven

Widen My Vision

God, open my eyes so I may see
And feel Your presence close to me.
Widen the vision of my unseeing eyes
So in passing faces I'll recognize
Not just a stranger, unloved and unknown,
But a friend with a heart that is much like my own.

Peace

If we but had the eyes to see
  God's face in every cloud,
If we but had the ears to hear
  His voice above the crowd,
If we could feel His gentle touch
  in every springtime breeze
And find a haven in His arms
  'neath sheltering, leafy trees,
If we could just lift up our hearts
  like flowers to the sun
And trust His loving promise
  and pray, "Thy will be done,"
We'd find the peace we're seeking,
  the kind no man can give—
The peace that comes from knowing
  He died so we might live!

Memories

Tender little memories
    of some word or deed
Give us strength and courage
    when we are in need.
Precious little memories
    of little things we've done
Make each day together
    a bright and happy one.
Blessed little memories
    of happiness and love
Are gifts to keep forever
    from our Father up above.

Shared Dreams

In my eyes there lies no vision
   but the sight of your dear face,
In my heart there is no feeling
   but the warmth of your embrace.
All my dreams are built around you,
   and I've come to know it's true,
In my life there is no living
   that is not a part of you.

Light in Your Eyes

The best things are nearest—
light in your eyes,
flowers at your feet,
duties at your hand,
the path of right just before you.
Then do not grasp at the stars,
but do life's plain, common work
as it comes,
certain that daily duties
and daily bread
are the sweetest things of life.